Ancient
Mexico

Ancient Mexico

An Overview

Jaime Litvak King

University of New Mexico Press
Albuquerque

Design by Milenda Nan Ok Lee

Library of Congress Cataloging in
Publication Data

Litvak King, Jaime.
Ancient Mexico, an overview.

   Bibliography: p.
   Includes index.
1. Indians of Mexico—Antiquities.
2. Indians of Mexico—History.
3. Mexico—Antiquities.
I. Title.
F1219.L73   1985   972'.01   85-1125

ISBN 0-8263-0817-1 (pbk.)

Contents

Figures

"Who are you?" said the Caterpillar.

This was not an encouraging opening for a conversation.

Alice replied, rather shyly, "I—I hardly know, sir, just at present—at least I know who I was when I got up this morning, but I think I must have changed several times since then."

Lewis Carroll, *Alice's Adventures in Wonderland*

Introduction

This book may look like a story about ruins and pyramids; about palaces, monuments, stelae, and sculpture; perhaps about religion and art; or about ritual and sacrifice; maybe even about gods, kings, priests, and warriors. It isn't. It is about ordinary people like you or me, and what they did, what they achieved, and what they believed.

These people lived a few years back and did not have a number of the conveniences we have today. They lived without such large animals as horses or cows that could be used for transport or for food. They didn't use

1

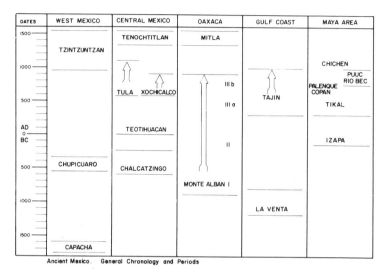

DATES	WEST MEXICO	CENTRAL MEXICO	OAXACA	GULF COAST	MAYA AREA
1500	TZINTZUNTZAN	TENOCHTITLAN	MITLA		CHICHEN
1000					PUUC RIO BEC
500		TULA XOCHICALCO	III b / III a	TAJIN	PALENQUE COPAN / TIKAL
AD 0 BC		TEOTIHUACAN	II		IZAPA
500	CHUPICUARO	CHALCATZINGO	MONTE ALBAN I		
1000				LA VENTA	
1500	CAPACHA				

Ancient Mexico.   General Chronology and Periods

Figure 1. General chronology, showing the time span for sites in the different regions of Mesoamerica. Note the contemporaneity of some of the most important sites and regional developments. (Drafted by Fernando Bolas)

metal for tools but only for ornament. They never used the wheel for work though they knew it as the shape of the sun, and they were able nevertheless to build pyramids, monuments, stelae, and sculpture. Their accomplishments were many despite a limited technology: they conceived a powerful and complicated religion with many gods to explain the workings of the universe and life, they developed an impressive art, surrounded their life with awesome, lush ritual that included human sacrifice, and evolved a society with kings, priests and warriors as well as commoners and slaves.

Not only that. When their world suddenly collapsed, in the sixteenth century, because they collided with another culture, their legacy was so rich that our life today contains many products and concepts that can be traced to them. So, as you see, this book is not just about people but about things and ideas as well.

The Humble Beginnings

2

Imagine another planet—one where the dominating species, the human race, having settled it from our own world, lived in isolation for thousands of years and had to develop its own way of life, with no help from others. That imaginary civilization is comparable to pre-European America. After crossing into the new land and after their retreat to Asia was cut off by the rising waters of the North Pacific and the Arctic Ocean, the in-migrants, hunters and gatherers, spread over the whole continent. Advancing south, as they were permitted by the terrain, they found new places to live and settle, adapted to new situations, and increased their numbers until the whole land mass, all the way to its extreme south end, the Tierra del Fuego, was populated.

These people were, to our way of thinking, savages. Their tools for coping with environment, animals, and weather were primitive, even if we compare them to what was being made in Western Europe at the time (twenty-five or thirty thousand years ago). They had a few crude scrapers and choppers, made of flint or some other stone that could be worked by a hard, well-placed tap, some sticks with their ends sharpened and hardened by fire, and bones, honed until they were pointy. It was not a lot to work with, but they managed. For more than twenty thousand years they struggled merely to assure survival, but they finally made it.

The key to survival was adaptation. Their tools had to be made from available materials, and these did not always permit the use of the familiar shapes they had brought from their homelands. The animals they hunted and the plants they gathered must have tasted new and strange. Their old legends and world view no longer explained the current circumstances of life, and new ones were developed to answer questions about why things were as they now were: the origin of the world, the shape and behavior of nature, and the very existence of their group.

They became isolated from other groups. Distances were great, and natural barriers made contact difficult. They were certainly too busy just surviving to have time for distant social calls. Although some common elements survived, they lost memory of the world from where they came. New words were added to speech since the old language did not have enough for the new experiences. Independent, small changes that occurred in the sounds of language were restricted to the group. In time, new languages, different from others, evolved. They even started to diverge physically. The traits of dominant individuals, those who were successful and had, therefore, a better opportunity to mate and did so more often, started to become more

Figure 2. A rather heroic rendering of the cornering of a mammoth in the National Museum of Anthropology, Mexico City. The depiction of prehistoric man in America as the killer of giant beasts has not been proven by archaeological finds. Although hunters may have taken a large animal once in a while, their camp remains show that they probably depended more on rabbits and other small rodents than on bigger game.

common until they became the norm. Some groups ended up taller or smaller, with longer or shorter noses, combining elements that were vital for survival with those that were merely the looks of their ancient sires. The diversity of ancient America, cultural as well as biological, was real.

These ancient Americans were those we call the mammoth hunters, although they probably spent more time hiding from the beasts than hunting them. While they did get to kill one of the monsters once in a while, most probably it was an aged, half-starved animal mired in the mud of a swamp or one that had slid off a hillside. They fed on anything killable by their scant armory—rodents, deer, coyotes, and rabbits—and on any plants they could gather—grasses, berries, roots, nuts, or fruits.

They were messy eaters, too. The remains of their prey, together with broken pieces of the stone implements used for the hunt and butchering, are found all over the continent. Some of their most important sites are Folsom, in the southwestern United States; Tepexpán and Santa Isabel Ixtapán, in the Valley of Mexico; and El Inga, in Ecuador. In time their flints became more and more efficient. Side notches were knapped for tighter binding to a wooden staff and for bleeding the prey. Today these implements are looked upon as art.

The Hunter Becomes a Farmer

Man is an intelligent creature. Given time he will find out about the world around him and learn how to use it to his advantage. The ancient Americans did it wherever they lived. They got to know what plants grew where and when they were at their best for gathering; where animals could be caught and fish trapped and the best time for these activities; where good stone for tools and reeds for baskets could be found. Eventually life became ruled by this knowledge.

The process of learning was slow and very probably as dependent on accident as on intention. Some care

3

was taken in picking the best plants, and possibly after some weeding the vegetables became bigger, more nutritious, and more dependent on human presence to survive and thrive, like corn in Mexico and manioc and potato in South America. Some predators, like the wild dog, found they could make a good living by keeping close to human habitation and scavenging for leftovers. Some birds, like the turkey and the parrot, were easy to catch and got used to captivity and being fed by humans.

So, about eight thousand years ago, the greatest revolution in human history was happening. Man in America was accomplishing the same task as his kin in the Near East and Southeast Asia. The hunters were becoming farmers. This was going on, independently, in North America, in Mexico and Central America, and in South America, with different peoples, using different resources.

In the dry highlands people domesticated corn and turkeys; in the lush, humid lowlands they grew manioc and tobacco; in the cold Andean mountains, the potato and the llama. In many places the crops were beans and squash. Temporary stopovers became permanent settlements if the land around them was good for growing. Clay became important first for waterproofing baskets and later, when people learned how to work it and harden it, for making into baked pots. Fibers could be woven and made into cloth, nets, ropes, and string.

Life had changed. Man could now predict his future. His food supply was assured so he could get on with the business of living. Housing could now be conceived as more than a cave shelter or a hut. Dress would become more than protection from the weather. There was now idle time. Time for inventing, for art, and for getting to know neighbors.

The Peddler as a Nobleman

4

The size of man's world is measured by what supports life. If we take a look at what we wear, what we eat, what we use, we will see the size of our world. We wear Swiss watches made in Taiwan, Italian ties made in the Philippines, African beads cast in San Francisco. We eat Caribbean pineapples grown in Hawaii, Southeast Asian bananas from Central America, Angus beef from Australia. No matter where we are we drink Scottish liquor, Chinese tea, Mexican beer, and Brazilian coffee. Our products are made by German or American machines. We drive

Japanese automobiles, watch British movies, and smell French perfume. Through travel we live in the whole world and our world is, indeed, the whole globe. But what was the world for a farmer in Central or Southern Mexico in the year 2,000 B.C.?

For one thing, it was known. People had settled many places in very early times, and towns had risen. To man this part of the world must have been home, since his kin had been living in those towns for a long time. Settled, farmer populations had existed in Tlapacoya, in the Valley of Mexico, by 4,000 B.C., and people who are now considered the possible ancestors of the Maya had been in Belize about that long.

Man's world was small. He had control over his environment and therefore was able to extract from it a great deal. But, to be able to do so, he had to specialize. In the same way that we today seek help rather than repair our own plumbing, or leave to others the science of healing, or import many of our staple items from other places where they can be grown or made better and cheaper, so too in Ancient

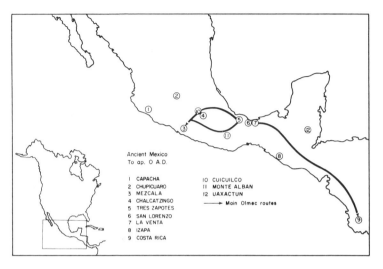

Figure 3. Ancient Mexico during the Preclassic Period (before c. A.D. 0). The arrows show the general line of Olmec influence that, by transporting goods produced in one area to other places, was probably the critical factor in the establishment of the Mesoamerican culture area. (Map by Fernando Bolas)

The Peddler as a Nobleman   17

Mexico did people devote themselves to some activities in preference to others.

In their towns, therefore, somebody else, perhaps one who had the natural ability, was the woodworker, potter, or stonecutter. This social mechanism, specilization, enabled a man to get good quality even if he himself could not make all the things he needed. He must have depended on others even for his spiritual life—makers, healers, shamans with good communication with the gods or spirits, better musicians, and better painters.

But life in town was certainly limited in many ways. Since the inhabitants worked a specific environment and only that environment, the assortment of goods, foodstuffs, textiles, and raw materials available must have been quite restricted, making daily life drab, to say the least. Of course some trading must have been carried on with neighboring groups, at least between wars, and raiding the neighbors brought goods that were not to be had locally. If you were on a valley bottom you could expect to get things from the hillsides or even from the next valley, which was lower or higher than yours and therefore produced a somewhat different range of products. But you went no farther; the world was small.

Allow me an aside. One of the most attractive traits of archaeology for most people, is that it resembles a real-life detective story. It starts out with a mystery. When the gallant explorers finish their work, it is solved; all loose ends are neatly tied together and the reader knows what happened. As an archaeologist let me tell you that it isn't so at all; archaeology doesn't even start out that way. It really begins not with a mystery but with the destruction of false knowledge.

There have always been explanations for archaeological remains. Folk legends tell about the miracles of saints, the work of races of giants or strangers from afar. National pride will refer to folk heroes. Modern pseudoscience will point to flying saucers and extraterrestrial beings. The archaeologist starts out by being very

interested in these tales, but what he *really* wants to learn is whether he can identify a few potsherds and assign to them a time and a cultural identity. Are they similar to some others, known from another place?

This is not as easy, or as romantic, as it sounds. It is hard and often rather boring work. But it does give you firm, solid knowledge instead of lore. And what is more, it is at the end of this process, not at the beginning, that you encounter a real, deeply interesting, mystery for the new knowledge leaves loose ends. If and when in the future the mystery is solved, it will not tie things together neatly but will beget a new and even more interesting puzzle. That is the real charm of archaeology: not what old mysteries it solves but what new ones it poses.

Figure 4. Capacha pottery. Found at the Capacha site, dating at 1750 B.C., were pots in shapes that were popular at a much later date in the Valley of Mexico, in Morelos, and in the northern part of Guerrero. This shows how styles travel and endure in large areas. (Isabel Kelly, *Ceramic Sequence in Colima: Capacha, an Early Phase,* p. 64)

This is the case with a site, in western Mexico, in the state of Colima, called Capacha. It was explored by a charming lady, Isabel Kelly, for the University of California. It is not an impressive place at all. Its remains include squash-shaped vessels and some other traits that show up in Central Mexico in sites dated from 800 to 1,200 B.C. Capacha, on the other hand, seems to date at about 1,750 B.C. Little is known of the period or the territory. What happened?

The possibilities are interesting. What went on in Capacha? Are we seeing the takeoff of a culture that was much more advanced than the rest of the area or just the work of some artisans who had a few good ideas that sold well? Are we facing two instances where the same thing was invented twice? Was Capacha a focus for development on the west coast, about 800 years before other people on the Gulf began to link different regions and built the Mesoamerican Culture area? How did those forms survive for almost a millennium? How did they get to Central Mexico? Are the dates believable?

That is the new mystery. Capacha has been written up in a very fine report by Dr. Kelly and is the new puzzle for Ancient Mexico. Future work may tell us what the site means, and it will probably be very important. The significance of Capacha may have to do with the very definition of Mesoamerica and the setting of geographical limits for the whole area.

Enter the Olmec, a people about whom we know very little. Their name, meaning the People from the Land of Rubber, was given by modern archaeologists. Their first traces seem to come from the southern coast of the Gulf of Mexico at about 1,200 B.C., when they already were a highly developed culture. According to a current theory espoused by Gareth Lowe, an archaeologist with Brigham Young University, the Olmec may be related to the Zoque, a people who live today in the northern part of the Mexican state of Chiapas. Very few Olmec sites have been dug, partly because of the difficulties of working in a rain forest. Drilling for oil is erasing the remains of the Olmec today.

Figure 5. Head number 3, found in the
southern Veracruz Preclassic site of San
Lorenzo Tenochtitlán, is very similar to pieces
found at La Venta, in the state of Tabasco.
Now housed at the Jalapa Archaeological
Museum, the sculpture is a massive andesite
stone weighing more than nine tons. Southern
Vercruz and western Tabasco correspond
approximately to the Olmec metropolitan area.
Olmec sculptured heads have been interpreted
as having negroid features, but skeletal
evidence does not support this idea. (*Historia
del arte mexicano* SALVAT 2:99)

We may never get the information
we need about their origins.

But we do know a few things about
the Olmec. Their white-rimmed black
pottery is a good marker, and it
followed their routes. They erected
some of the most impressive
monuments in antiquity. The stone
heads, probably of their rulers, show
flat-nosed, thick-lipped, round-
headed, heavy-browed men who have
sometimes been tagged as negroid.
They were not. Their skeletons have
been studied. Bones and art show that
the Olmec had no curly hair, no long
heads, no protruding teeth or alveoli.
They hewed their statues in basalt, a
rock that could be found some fifty or
sixty miles from their towns and could
be transported by raft on some of the
region's many rivers.

The Olmec could also have been the
inventors, or more likely the
disseminators, of an ancient
numbering system—a dot for one and
a bar for five—that might have
included a positional system for units
of twenty. It was a very efficient way
of working with numbers. A later
people, the Maya, who added a

beanlike character for zero, were able to do wonderful calculations for astronomical purposes. But numbers were, before anything else, required for trade.

They seem to have been concerned with a religion that deified the jaguar, some crocodile-like reptile, and a snake. Their art shows not only sculptures of the beasts but also their synthesized features: cross-like markings, crests, and fangs. These designs are also seen as ornaments in dress, helmets, and tatoos. Their belief focused on rain and water, with raindrops and water signs abundant in their representations, a natural thing for people who depended on agriculture for their very existence. Olmec art also includes depictions of an odd being: a human with a mouth downturned at the lip edges, sometimes with the head split longitudinally as if axed in two. Interpretations of this persona range from a werejaguar to a person afflicted with Downs' Syndrome.

The Olmec built the first pyramid in Ancient Mexico, sometime around 1,000 B.C. Not a very impressive

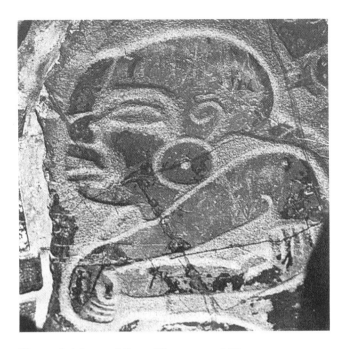

Figure 6. Monte Alban "Danzante." The settlement of Monte Alban dates from the Early Preclassic. Olmec-related figures such as the Danzantes include carved stones representing humans with features not unlike those of the colossal heads. These probably have to do with the presence of the Olmec as a cultural elite at Monte Alban. This site also features, much earlier than any other place in ancient Mexico, inscriptions with a vigesimal numerical system that was probably used locally and was picked up by the Olmec and, later, by all Mesoamerica. (L. de la Torre, *Historia del arte mexicano* SALVAT 2:68)

The Peddler as a Nobleman

Figure 7. A stone mosaic found at the Olmec site of La Venta. It has been interpreted as a schematized jaguar mask. Olmec art represents animals like the jaguar, the serpent, and the crocodile that could have been either totemic animals or animal advocations of the forces of nature. Olmec images are later used in most Mesoamerican cultures. (*Historia del art mexicano* SALVAT 1:35)

building, it looks like a partly successful attempt at playing with earth in a giant Jello mold. The pyramid was probably developed from a house mound, a means of keeping dry in a swampy area, and was not considered a ritual edifice until much later. The main Olmec sites, La Venta, in the state of Tabasco, where the pyramid was found, and San Lorenzo, in southern Veracruz, were great ceremonial centers in their time. Their contents can be viewed at the archaeological park in Villahermosa, the state capital of Tabasco, and in the museum in Jalapa, in Veracruz, neither of which is frequently visited but both of which have collections well worth looking at.

The Olmec were traders. They picked up local materials that could be used somewhere else and exchanged them for products from other lands. Their mark is the greenstone: the American jade that they carved masterfully into human figures and votive axes engraved with people with tiger mouths. They also traded in cinnabar, the red dust that was used to cover the dead and is now mined for its mercury. To get these minerals they had to go far. Their presence is noted in remains from central Mexico all the way to Costa Rica, deep in Central America.

Trade, not an easy occupation at any time, must have been incredibly difficult in ancient Mexico. No large animals were found by the original Asian immigrants, and the wheel had not been discovered. Loads had to be carried on the backs of men who, in turn, had to be fed and taken care of during extensive journeys. The carrying capacity of man is limited—a later source places it at about fifty pounds carried for about five or six hours a day—so only things that were very light or very expensive for their weight could be used in long-distance trading. A class of human beasts of burden developed, made obsolete some twenty-five hundred years later by the technology of the Spanish conquerors.

The Olmec must also have been caravaneers. Just as with the peddler in the development of the midwestern United States, their role was vital. They were the Sears, Roebuck catalog of their age. By carrying merchandise from one place to another they became important, even indispensable. When the Europeans arrived they reported that traders—the *pochteca* as the Aztec traders were called—were universally respected. To kill them or highjack their caravans was looked upon as a terrible crime and brought immediate and bloody revenge from armies they could support on their own.

Whatever else they achieved, the Olmec established the beginning of civilization in this part of the world. By linking regions together and making them dependent on products from afar, they started the high-culture area of Central and Southern Mexico and Northern Central America we now call Mesoamerica—the place where, later, great achievements were accomplished. Olmec paraphernalia— the feather flyswatter, the baton, and the X-shaped cross—became the symbols of high rank for future Mesoamerican rulers and the ancestors of future faiths. They were, as Alfonso Caso, the great Mexican archaeologist once put it, the Mother Culture. The peddler was a nobleman.

The City Dwellers

One more thing we do not know about the Olmecs is how they went offstage. By 500 B.C. they seem to have disappeared. Several possibilities exist. They could have mixed with the local populations in different places and, in their central habitat, they could have just declined. Their presence and power could have been made obsolete by other, more efficient traders who eliminated the high cost entailed by the search for jade. Their metropolitan area on the Gulf Coast could have been made redundant by routes that bypassed it and bypassed their culture, which therefore became

5

provincial. No matter how they perished, their culture traits persisted in many places, eventually appearing in later civilizations.

Some of the Olmec were the cultural ancestors of the Maya. The site of Izapa, in Chiapas, with its many plazas and pyramids, contains carved stelae which, because of their motifs and dates, could be considered Olmecoid. Many pieces from Izapa are in the museum at the state capital, Tuxtla Gutierrez, and some are in the National Museum in Mexico City. They show people rendering obeisance to rulers, and they are the direct antecedents of the Maya monuments. At Chalcatzingo, in the eastern part of the state of Morelos, near the resort city of Cuautla, one sees impressive rock carvings in the Olmec style showing mythical monsters and a ruler sitting on a throne.

Whatever finally happened to the Olmec, their presence shook up

Figure 8. Stela 21, Izapa, seems to show a sacrifice by decapitation. Olmec features are the sky and the hanging water drops. (*Historia del arte mexicano* SALVAT 2:126)

Mesoamerica. The fact that theirs was a trading domain rearranged settlement. Some towns became collection and distribution points for trade goods. The use of human carriers made frequent stops necessary, and from the stopping places, local market sites developed. These places were at an advantage for future development. They were centrally located in their regions, and their position as trade centers made them the best places for other activities.

Because a relatively large population passed through them, surplus wealth could be found in these towns. They became places where artisans could easily be engaged by their customers, and these towns became the industrial and manufacturing sites for their regions. As a result, their population increased. They were, of course, the natural seats for government, since they were good places from which to regulate movement and tap riches. Religion found its flock in those towns and they became important ceremonial centers.

Economic activity, civil authority,

and religious ritual begot a permanent metropolis. Temples, rich houses, and wide squares were the result. Cuicuilco, about a mile south of the campus of the University of Mexico, with its huge round pyramid, is a good example. At many sites, the middleman functions of service and manufacturing activities became central; agricultural and mining products could be had by trading. The villages became cities and their inhabitants became sophisticated urbanites. Civilization had arrived.

Although it may be safely stated that the development of the city in Mesoamerica stemmed from the effect of the Olmec—even in places they had not reached—other groups had also become traders and built cities. West Mexico, a region about which we know very little, seems to have experienced these phenomena. From possible beginnings in a sequence that started with Capacha there developed, in the southern part of the state of Guanajuato, near the lake region of Michoacán, a culture we call Chupicuaro after its main site. Chupicuaro seems to have been a very

Figure 9. Polychrome pottery from Chupicuaro, a west Mexican site in the state of Guanajuato, now covered by a dam, shows a stylistic resemblance to pieces from the southwestern United States. Some figurines are flat, with slanted eyes and pasted-on features; later pieces are modeled. The polychrome decoration may represent body paint. The site dates from a period after the decline of the Olmec, with whom there is no evidence of contact, and its influence extended to the Valley of Mexico. (*Historia del arte mexicano* SALVAT 2:7)

Ancient Mexico

important trade and manufacturing center for ceramic figures and vases on which black-and-white lines were painted on a highly polished red background.

Chupicuaro influence spread throughout the area, reaching even into Central Mexico and somehow up to the southwestern United States. It was probably the origin of other achievements in Western Mexico up to and including those of the much later Tarascans. However, the most important Chupicuaro site, the one that developed into what could be called the capital of Mesoamerica, was a settlement on the site where later stood the magnificent city of Teotihuacán, in the northern Valley of Mexico.

Gods and Giants

In its time, from about A.D. 100 to 750, Teotihuacán was the undisputed center of Mesoamerican life. In its heyday it was the largest city in the world, not just in Mesoamerica. It came to have more than 125,000 inhabitants and dominated all of the area's territory. The Aztecs, who found it already in ruins, were so impressed that they believed that giants had built it. The presence of mammoth bones nearby reinforced this notion and, according to local legend, the ruined, holy place was where the gods met to create the world. Teotihuacán, in English, means

6

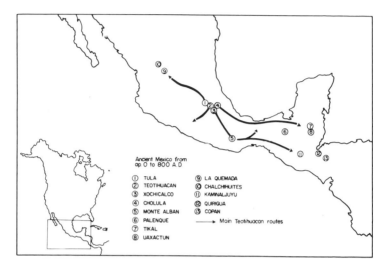

Figure 10. Mesoamerica during the Classic Period, c. A.D. 0–800. Arrows show the line of Teotihuacán influence that, stemming from Teotihuacán's control of the obsidian trade, came to dominate the exchange network throughout the area. Teotihuacán's rule went substantially unchallenged until the Late Classic. (Map by Fernando Bolas)

The Place Where Gods Were Made.

The city itself is certainly impressive. The long Avenue of the Dead, the Pyramids of the Sun and the Moon, the huge Ciudadela compound—probably the rulers' household—are built in a unique monumental style. Teotihuacan's art, featuring the sculptured heads of snakes and of the Rain God coming out of the side of a stepped building, mythical animals both bird and butterfly, murals of parading felines, of healers and patients, and even of a garden with streams and fountains, with people in song and play— probably one of their paradises— makes it one of the world's most magnificent examples of human achievement.

Teotihuacán signifies a complete transformation of Mesoamerican life. Not only does it show the change from village to great city but also, in religion, it represents the coming of age of the early fertility cults and their development into a formalized way of belief. In its art one can see the development of a specific rain god, later the Aztec Tlaloc, with special

Figure 11. Teotihuacán, the great Classic site in the Valley of Mexico. The photo is taken from the Pyramid of the Moon, which was excavated in the seventeenth century, probably the first archaeological excavation in Mesoamerica. The Avenue of the Dead, which runs down the middle of the photo, marks a north-south axis across the ceremonial area. To the east (left) is the Pyramid of the Sun, the tallest structure at the site. The ruler's household, the Ciudadela, is hidden behind that structure. Teotihuacán was the great node for the communications network in Mesoamerica during the Classic Period, and also controlled the obsidian traffic. Teotihuacán was a regional power until about A.D. 750, by which time its control over trade had ebbed. (Photo by William M. Ferguson and John Q. Royce)

Figure 12. West facade of the Pyramid of Quetzalcoatl, Teotihuacán. This temple is located in the Ciudadela compound. The figures that stick out represent gods that probably originated in the Early Classic Period but were worshiped—certainly with substantial changes in their meaning—until the Spanish conquest. The Aztecs knew these gods as Quetzalcoatl (the Feathered Snake) and Tlaloc (the Rain God). The background is made of the snakes' bodies and water-related motifs. (*Historia del arte mexicano* SALVAT 2:11)

attributes and formal characteristics, and his link with another deity, Quetzalcoatl, the Feathered Snake, who probably started as a culture hero and became an important god by himself.

But even more impressive is the evidence of Teotihuacán's power. It shows the end product of a progression in social organization from dispersion to centralized strength. In many ways it is the perfect example of the road from local appropriation to a continental-scale use of the environment, and it compares with the domains of the most important Asian or European empires of antiquity.

How do we see the power of countries like America or Japan and of cities like New York or Hong Kong? There are armies, of course, and embassies and flags. But even more important are the products made there and found as originals or copies all over the world, cars, machines, furniture, appliances, and innumerable other items that are made in many different places but are imitations or developments from American, Japanese, or other originals. Influence on this scale can also be seen, in Mesoamerica, for Teotihuacán.

Its pottery, a thin orange ware and a brown, cylindrical, stick-polished vessel is found throughout Mesoamerica, exported from the original site and copied locally. So is its characteristic style of construction, a short inclined embankment with a large vertical wall extending from it. In some places, like Monte Alban, in the state of Oaxaca, the building style developed a shape of its own but was still clearly a Teotihuacán-influenced product. At Tikal, in the Maya heartland of lowland Guatemala, stelae proudly show the effigy of the Teotihuacán Rain God as protector and amulet for their own rulers, who trace their descent from a Teotihuacán-bred dynasty. All of Mesoamerica looked upon Teotihuacán as its center.

The formula for earthly power, though, must be somewhat like the one for gravity, in direct proportion to mass and inverse to the square of distance. No matter how big and powerful the metropolis was, it could not reach directly to the far ends of its domain. The walking distance between

Figure 13. The influence of the great Classic metropolis of the Valley of Mexico is shown by the distribution of pottery like this piece from Teotihuacán, and by the number of local imitations in this style. It is a fine ware with almost cylindrical walls and painted and incised decoration. (I. Marquina, *Arquitectura Prehispanica*)

Figure 14. Tikal, located in the Peten, Guatemala, is the earliest large development in the Maya Classic Period. Its pyramids, topped with their peculiar roof combs, are grouped in acropoloi, and its plazas are decorated with stelae that sometimes show figures of high position with Teotihuacán-style ornamentation on their dress. This is a view of Temple A, or Temple I. (Photo by William M. Ferguson and John Q. Royce)

Central Mexico and the Maya area is close to two months. News of anything that might happen on the periphery of the Teotihuacán-ruled area would require a period of many days to travel to the metropolis; only then could the central power do something about it. The city's power was undermined by its own success in empire building.

Besides, as with the Olmec, Teotihuacán's real power was trade—in this case mainly the control of obsidian. A society without metal has to find other materials to cut and pierce, and in Mesoamerica the material of choice was obsidian, the green translucent stone that was found in the mountains near the modern-day city of Pachuca, in the state of Hidalgo. This monopoly gave the metropolis the key to almost unlimited power and with it control over the whole Mesoamerican area. The result was creation of a gigantic web that centered on the site with component regions bringing in their products and tribute for the profit of the great capital.

Whatever one believes, distance in

human culture is not a factor of space but rather of time; the distance to a place is really how long it takes to get there. In a culture that never developed the wheel and never had access to the horse, time was especially critical. To develop power Teotihuacán had to allow, even promote, the growth of regional distributors, sites where large-scale trading could be done and that also could serve as relays for the trade network.

These regional distributors were the great Classic sites: Monte Alban, the Veracruz Coast, Kaminaljuyu in the Guatemalan highlands, and the Peten sites in the lowlands. In the north Chalchihuites and La Quemada, in Zacatecas, and many other places became the main centers for the distribution of Teotihuacán trade in objects and ideas. With trade they prospered and became important culture centers of their own, in some ways surpassing the splendor of the metropolis.

Of these other cultures, the Maya were able not only to develop their Olmec-descended calendar, used in

Figure 15. The Valley of Oaxaca, from Monte Alban. The site dominates its immediate environment. Monte Alban probably began as a local center. As the Teotihuacán trade network extended to the south and west, Monte Alban became an important link on its routes and a local distributor of Teotihuacán influence. (Photo by William M. Ferguson and John Q. Royce)

Figure 16. The Central Plaza, Monte Alban. The ceremonial center is on the leveled top of a high hill. Begun in the Preclassic, Monte Alban reached its apex as a powerful settlement in the Early Classic Period. It was used until the Spanish conquest as a burial ground, and some of the site's most impressive finds come from this use. (Photo by William M. Ferguson and John Q. Royce)

Figure 17. This Tzakol polychrome pot, with concave sides, a basal flange, and three hemispheric supports, is a good example of a type of pottery that can be followed throughout the southern Maya Classic Period. (*Historia del arte mexicano* SALVAT 2:118)

Figure 18. Palenque, in the state of Chiapas, is located where the Gulf Coast plain meets the slope that becomes the Sierra Madre. Palenque's florescence in the Late Classic Period was probably due to its role as a trading link between the coastal and mountain regions. It was probably destroyed and occupied by Totonac invaders, whose pottery is found on the ruins. The building at left is the Palace, with the Temple of Inscriptions to the right. (Photo by William M. Ferguson and John Q. Royce)

complicated astronomy to predict the movement of stars and planets for personal horoscopes and omens, but also to create their glyphic system of writing, which told of the deeds of local rulers. Also, closer to the Olmec tradition, the Maya carved facades and statues with the same themes.

In Oaxaca, the fortified site of Monte Alban showed a high degree of city planning and astronomical knowledge. In the Central Veracruz area, a style of stone and clay sculpture developed that is notable for its realistic representations. In Central Mexico, the cities of Cholula, where the tallest pyramid in Mesoamerica was eventually erected, and Xochicalco, the fortress city of the South, watched over its routes of approach.

The Teotihuacán-linked settlements

Figure 19. One of the easternmost Maya sites, Copán flourished during Late Classic times. It was a trade center of the Motagua River valley. Stela C, like other stelae, portrays a chieftain, with dates that are associated with various events in his life. (Photo by William M. Ferguson and John Q. Royce)

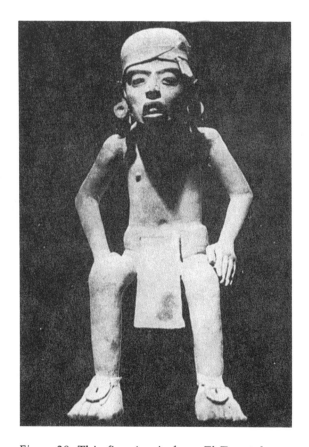

Figure 20. This figurine is from El Zapotal, a Late Classic site in Central Vercruz that shows stylistic influence from several other regions, especially Teotihuacán. El Zapotal pottery is remarkable for its lifelike shapes. This figure is made in two sections and can be disassembled at the waist. (Photo by N. Gutierrez in *Historia del arte mexicano* SALVAT 2:115)

Figure 21. Cholula, near the city of Puebla, was settled throughout most of the Mesoamerican sequence and survived the fall of the central Mexican Classic Period. It remained an important city until the Spanish conquest. (Photo by William M. Ferguson and John Q. Royce)

grew and prospered. They became great cities in their own right. But their efficiency as distributors for the network started to wane as they consumed more and more of the surplus until finally none was flowing toward the metropolis. At about A.D. 650 Teotihuacán's undisputed domain was just its immediate surroundings, the Valley of Mexico. The large, nonproductive population of Teotihuacán could not subsist on such meager fare. The city's power was gone and with it its splendor.

Whether Teotihuacán's final fall was due to invasion, civil strife, or a combination of both along with other factors is not known. By the year 750 it was gone and burned. People, living on the ruins, were no longer working the green obsidian; instead, they used a coarser, local, grey kind. The giants were dead.

Chaos and Rebirth

7

The fall of Teotihuacán must have been the most cataclysmic event in Mesoamerica prior to the coming of the Europeans. Many of the great cities that had been linked to the trade routes withered and died, some immediately and others after a while. Those that were irretrievably linked to the center collapsed quickly; others survived for a time.

The southern Maya cities were extinguished slowly, probably with the help of wars and uncertain ruling lineages. According to Harvard archaeologist Gordon Willey, A.D. 600 marked the beginning of a strange,

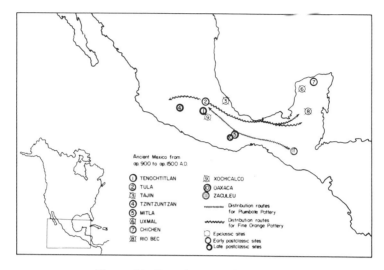

Figure 22. Postclassic Mesoamerica, c. A.D. 900–1500. Arrows indicate the distribution of two types of pottery that were widely traded. The Aztecs eventually dominated most of the northern part of the area. (Map by Fernando Bolas)

static phase in their culture that probably coincides with their disconnection from Teotihuacán. The marker stelae stopped being made by about the year 1000 at the latest. By then, the head of the Rain God was shown on prisoners, not on kings. Art at sites like Bonampak, in Chiapas, shows battles, perhaps against non-Maya foes. In the Honduran site of Copán, a local ruler—Sunrise is his glyphic name—acquired a reputation as a warrior while defending the border to the south.

In Central Mexico some settlements made a bid to inherit Teotihuacán's power. Xochicalco had its most glorious century when it was no longer subservient to Teotihuacán. Great palaces and the Pyramid of the Serpents, with its reliefs of feathered snakes and carved personages in Maya costume, are from this period, when it attempted to fill the old city's role. Xochicalco's glory did not last. Although its influence extended through the Balsas River region and even touched the Puebla-Tlaxcala valley, where murals in Cacaxtla show terrible battles in a very realistic

Figure 23. Tajin, in northern Veracruz, survived the end of the Classic and was active in the early Postclassic Period. Its design showed influence from the Huasteca culture to the north, as well as from Teotihuacán. The Pyramid of Niches could be linked with some sort of calendric concept since it contains 365 niches. (Photo by William M. Ferguson and John Q. Royce)

Figure 24. The site of Río Bec, in the southern part of the state of Campeche, is connected to the northern expansion of the Classic Maya after the fall of Teotihuacán. (Photo by William M. Ferguson and John Q. Royce)

Chaos and Rebirth   65

painting style, it lacked the power base to go farther.

The northern border collapsed under the first of several invasions by hunters from the semidesert northern plains. Thin Orange pottery was no longer distributed and in the Valley of Mexico and surroundings a new ware, Coyotlatelco red-on-buff, marks the narrow range of the safe distribution of goods at the time. Not everything died, though. The northern Maya, no longer limited by their former subservience to Teotihuacán, thrived. They developed new sites, places like Kohunlich, Xpuhil, and Becán in the states of Quintana Roo and Campeche and, in time, the cities of Edzna, Sayil, Labna, Kabah, and the great Uxmal, with their own style, no longer linked to the old tradition of building. A new Long-Nosed God substituted in many ways for the old cult of Itzamna.

Figurines made on the island of Jaina, off the coast of Campeche, are distributed throughout the region and beyond, and a pigment, Maya blue, made of a material found only in the peninsula of Yucatán, is present in murals and pottery even as far away

Figure 25. Sayil, in southern Yucatán, is an early Puuc settlement. It features a three-story building with columns. (Photo by William M. Ferguson and John Q. Royce)

Figure 26. Uxmal, in southern Yucatán, is probably the largest site dating from the late Puuc period, just before the onset of Toltec influence in the Maya area. (Photo by William M. Ferguson and John Q. Royce)

as Central Mexico, in Xochicalco-influenced sites. Such wide distribution is good evidence of the prosperity of both the surviving and the new Maya cities of that time, and of the links among them. It is possible that Veracruz-based traders were influential in such connections. From the time of Teotihuacán's fall, hegemony over all of Mesoamerica by any one site was never again possible.

As much as any group, however, the northern Maya must have been close to becoming a paramount power in the area. In the period between A.D. 900 and 1000 trade goods, at least those that remain for archaeologists to examine, were coming mainly from the south.

Maya flowering at that time is attested by the distribution of two ceramic types. The first is Fine Orange, an unslipped plainware that seems to have originated east of the region where the Olmec culture had its center and that was occupied by Maya-speaking groups in later days. Fine Orange ware seems to have been distributed from a very interesting site, Champotón, near the mouth of the Laguna de Terminos, in southern Campeche, a place that became an important port of trade between the Maya and the rest of Mesoamerica. Fine Orange had a predominantly Maya distributuion and showed the extent of trade between Maya groups. It has been found in large quantities throughout the Yucatán Peninsula, all the way to its northern edge, where Teotihuacán wares never reached. It also was found in the Central Gulf Coast and, in lesser quantities, Central Mexico.

The other important ware is called Plumbate, a metallic looking, high-temperature ceramic type shaped in animal and human figures. It was made near the southern Mexico-Guatemala border and was distributed from there throughout Mesoamerica, even reaching into West Mexico. It has the widest distribution of any ceramic type made in pre-Hispanic Mesoamerica and heralded the rebirth of the area as a unified region. This unification, certainly a weaker linking of the component regions than had been achieved through the once overwhelming presence of

Teotihuacán, seems to have been controlled, again from Central Mexico, through the Toltec.

According to their own legends, the Toltec were a hunting folk who came into Mesoamerica at the time of the fall of Teotihuacan. Eventually they took over some of its former domain and seem to have exerted quite an influence even into the southeast. They are characterized archaeologically by the presence of flat figurines and by a red-on-buff ware we call Mazapa, a rather badly made ware with dishes whose designs resemble, though we do not know why, some of the motifs that were prevalent, at the time, in the American Southwest.

After about A.D. 900 or 1000 archaeology and its materials are no longer our only source of information. Many of our data come from ethnohistory, including local legends and folklore, and are therefore more liable to human, subjective distortion. The Toltec, in Aztec traditions, are described in a heroic scale. They are master sorcerers, great artists, clever engineers, and inspired poets. Rulers, in Maya legends, acquire nobility by being anointed by the Toltec, and Aztec dynasties claimed them as ancestors.

All this splendor is not backed by archaeology. The Toltec capital, Tula, in the state of Hidalgo north of Mexico City, started out as a Teotihuacán settlement and grew into a rather large city at around A.D. 900. Nothing in real life could ever compare with the ethnohistoric descriptions of the place. To make a point, although Beijing is a great city, "In Xanadu did Kubla Khan . . ." is not a very precise visitor's guide for it.

Figure 27. North of Mexico City, in the state of Hidalgo, was Tula, the capital city of the Toltec people, whom the Aztecs considered their cultural ancestors. The location of the Toltec city was a matter of much discussion until chronologies were refined and the identity of Tula in that role was accepted in the late 1930s. Although legends describe the fall of Tula, it was an important center at the time of the Spanish conquest. These figure-columns are located on top of the pyramid of Tlahuizcalpantecuhtli, dedicated to the planet Venus, the evening star. The building's resemblance to structures at Chichén Itzá is an argument for Toltec influence at the latter site. (Photo by William M. Ferguson and John Q. Royce)

Some of the might of Tula, to be sure, must have been real. In many ways the Toltec were the inheritors of the Teotihuacán mantle. They certainly must have ruled Central Mexico and parts beyond. Their pottery and their figurines, with dresses that resemble the most elaborate styles of the former capital, have a wide distribution. Tula seems to be the center of distribution, in its own area and toward West Mexico, of the Maya-made Fine Orange and Plumbate wares. The controversial finding, in the Maya city of Chichén Itzá, in the Yucatán Peninsula, of Toltec-type buildings certainly points toward their influence far away from their home turf.

Toltec culture and power and their extent are interesting and important subjects. The dissolution of the Teotihuacán trade network had left Mesoamerica a fragmented territory. Several towns made a bid for the heir's position, but each failed to sustain itself in that role; it was Tula, for a while, that possibly came nearest to succeeding. But the Toltec were no longer dominating a territory of feeder-villages and small market towns, as was the situation when the Teotihuacán control started to grow. By the end of the Classic, as the Teotihuacán-dominated period is called, many of these places had become magnificent, powerful centers on their own and had developed their own population structures. They had their own rulers, possibly the remains of Teotihuacán merchant groups, and a sure domination over their own, admittedly limited, territories.

Even more, the climatic diversity of the area, making for markedly different environments that produced different articles, along with the rugged Mesoamerican terrain, which made for difficulty in communication even between close neighbors, and the restraints of human-carried trade—all these resulted in isolated regions. Although elites could be quite close to each other because they were in constant contact through merchants whose products they could afford, the farmer inhabitants had slowly developed into specific, diversified ethnic groups.

Ethnicity emerges from separateness. Ethnic groups form

slowly as different population units, by acquiring particular culture traits, become distinct from their neighbors. Isolation is the key. Language, little by little, changes in a place by imperceptible steps, and eventually dialects of the same tongue become unintelligible to other speakers. And so it goes with other characteristics as well. Each group, from its own experience, develops a separate set of legends, of heroes, and its own history that distinguishes it as a unit. Groups acquire different mannerisms that develop into specific codes of conduct and often, even by miraculous revelations that are not shared with other peoples, develop separate religions—their own way of explaining the universe around them. The end result is a differentiated, often fiercely independent, human population, like those already formed at the time of Toltec expansion.

Furthermore, the fall of Teotihuacán, accompanied by deep social and political upheaving in the area, had other consequences. It also brought on the mobilization of populations. The fall of the northern border, for example, opened the area to the half-civilized hunters that lived there and unbalanced the demographic map. Some groups had to abandon their territories and find space in regions already occupied by others. In some places, like the Central Maya zone, at Altar de Sacrificios and Seibal, in Guatemala, we have evidence for the inclusion of Central Mexican, non-Teotihuacán materials that could mean warlike conquest. The Maya traditions speak of the coming of the Putuns, merchant folk from outside the region.

These movements, before the Toltec rose to power, go a long way toward explaining their emergence and success. Understanding the Toltec, though, has taken archaeologists a long time. The site of Chichén Itzá shows how archaeology is always in the process of reexamining its own findings. In this case the new ideas were provided by the work of two very young professionals. When the site was dug, in the 1920s, the resemblance of many of its buildings to others in Tula, the Toltec capital, was intriguing. The Yucatec site also had other monuments in the style of

Ancient Mexico

other Maya cities, edifices with the prominent representation of the Long-Nosed God. The explanation at the time seemed quite simple: a purely Maya period, the Puuc phase, was superseded by a Mexican-influenced epoch. The whole peninsula's sequence was neatly arranged to correspond with these two periods.

Today we are in doubt. New excavations, and a new look by Charles Lincoln, of Harvard University, at the evidence shows that the Toltec phenomenon is limited to Chichén itself and even there other buildings, in the older dated Puuc style, could be contemporaneous or even later than the Central Mexican-influenced monuments. It is still very tentative, but a good case seems to exist for the persistence of the old style through what was thought to be

Figure 28. The building known as the Church is a good example of non-Toltec architecture at Chichén Itzá. This building and others in the Puuc style are now seen as evidence for the coexistence of the two styles, which, in turn, suggests that the Toltecs did not completely dominate the Maya domain. (Photo by William M. Ferguson and John Q. Royce)

Figure 29. The Toltec aspect of Chichén Itzá is well represented by the structure known as the Castle, with its flat roof and stairways on each side. It has a substructure in the same style. (Photo by William M. Ferguson and John Q. Royce)

the later epoch. Thus Toltec influence has to be seen not as a period but rather as an intrusion within a period; it need not be explained by total conquest. A Toltec-ized Maya elite in one town could account for the phenomenon. A reexamination of the dates for the distribution of Plumbate and Fine Orange, by Bernd Fahmel, of the University of Mexico, bears this out and points toward further rearrangement of the sequence in other regions.

Why Playing Ball with the Gods is Dangerous

For archaeology as well as for the other historical sciences, the Toltec are a fascinating folk. This interest comes from their role in the development of the Mesoamerican culture but also, in central Mexico at least, because they were the first users of metal and possibly also the first wielders of the bow and arrow. These characteristics make them very intriguing indeed.

We do not really know who they were. They recognized themselves as speakers of Nahuatl, later spoken by the Aztec, a language of the family we call Uto-Aztecan that comprises many others in North Mexico and the

8

American Southwest. Indeed, in their own legends they tell of coming from the north under the leadership of their lord Mixcoatl, the Serpent of Smoke. But since it is quite possible that the same language was spoken in Teotihuacán, at least by the common people, they could just as well have been survivors of the great city's downfall and their version merely a tall tale, a not uncommon event in folk traditions.

They themselves told a legend of having been hunters who acquired, along the way, the power and polish that made them so influential in the development of the area. Mixcoatl's life was full of heroic and miraculous incidents and he was seen later, by the Aztec, as a god. A validation of their tradition is found in their having gods of a type not found before—solar hunters and warriors.

Figure 30. A column from the series on the west side of the Temple of the Warriors at Chichén Itzá. The warrior stands in full regalia with a huge quetzal-feather headdress. (William M. Ferguson and John Q. Royce, *Maya Ruins of Mexico in Color*)

Figure 31. Jaguars and eagles are depicted devouring human hearts in this low-relief panel on the south side of the Temple of the Warriors. The jaguar has a human heart in its paw while the eagle (right) has it in its claw. Both are posed to eat the heart. (William M. Ferguson and John Q. Royce, *Maya Ruins of Mexico in Color*)

The archaeological record for their origin is not clear. Although their Mazapa Red-on-Buff pottery is a good marker for time and ethnic provenience, other pottery types are not. Two more, also assigned to them, an orange brushed-on ceramic and a greyish brown ware with a white, easily lost slip, could be linked with other wares made during the Classic in the North Central states of Guanajuato and Queretaro.

If these wares are well placed, then their North, or possibly West Mexican origin, would be confirmed. But most of the rest of their culture, including much of their symbolism, is already found at Teotihuacán. Processions of tigers and eagles eating human hearts, many of their glyphs for dates, and even their building style can be traced to shapes from Teotihuacán to Xochicalco.

It is also most interesting that the Toltecs had metal. The craft of metalworking came very late to Mesoamerica. Our earliest dates for copper bells, from the coast of the state of Guerrero, are A.D. 900, hundreds of years after other culture areas had metal. It could have come from Central America. It was used almost exclusively for ornament and seems to have been first distributed from West Mexico until other regions learned the techniques to work it by themselves.

The impact of a given invention or discovery in a culture depends very much on how it is put to use. Because new inventions or products, owing to their scarcity or newness, are normally expensive, their use is usually limited to the elite. Many times they are assigned to a ritual or ceremonial context. Later they are found in more utilitarian contexts when the culture recognizes the possibility of using the new product or technology in other ways. The ability to recognize such applications is often a product of technological advance itself, a field where Mesoamerica had very clear limitations.

In spite of its other achievements, Mesoamerica was in fact never very advanced technologically. One of its notable lags was in the control of temperature. The art of building closed kilns and of controlling the air in them was never widespread. Pottery was normally baked in the open air, placing the raw pieces on or near an open fire. The product of this technique can never be as evenly fired as one made in a closed oven. Furthermore, temperature is never high enough for glazing. This problem, of course, limited metallurgists to soft metals such as copper, silver, and gold, which melt at relatively low temperatures and do not make very good tools.

Mesoamerican metals are now being very busily researched, and some writers believe that by the time of the conquest a breakthrough had been achieved with the production of true bronze by alloying tin and copper. If this was so, then tool making was not far away. The distribution of bronze, however, was not widespread, so bronze work was not common. Had it been, of course, Mesoamerica would have been very different in every way. As it was, metal objects were almost just another kind of stone ornament.

One Mesoamerican invention that was certainly important was the bow and arrow. Today, when we want to refer to a people as primitive we tag them as using the bow and arrow. This description is not apt, since the bow and arrow are quite a sophisticated weapon. In Mesoamerica they were introduced very late, probably at the time of the Toltec or, at the earliest, by the fall of Teotihuacán, surely from the North. The military advantage in reach, penetration, and accuracy of using this weapon over simply hurling projectiles is quite clear. Decisive in waging war, the bow and arrow represented a great advance in this art.

Earlier weapons, both for hunting and for war, were limited to lances, clubs, and a very interesting artifact, the dart-thrower or atlatl, a mechanical extension of the human arm that permitted a longer shot and, if well used, could be aimed quite accurately. It is even now used by duck hunters in Patzcuaro Lake, in Michoacán, and, until recently, by Eskimo seal hunters. In Mesoamerica it was represented in sculpture, and even in Toltec Tula it is shown, on the monumental statues on top of the main pyramid, as a ceremonial sidearm for military

Figure 32. From the Mapa Quinatzin, a depiction of the arrival of the Chichimecs. Enlarged here are scenes of the hunt using bow and arrow (top) and men with spear throwers (bottom).

Playing Ball with the Gods

Figure 33. Quetzalcoatl, the feathered serpent, was known to the Mayas as Kukulcán. Its representations are the most numerous at Chichén Itzá. (William M. Ferguson and John Q. Royce, *Maya Ruins of Mexico in Color*)

officers, very much like our use of the old-fashioned sabre today.

Toltec religion also shows important differences from Teotihuacán. The worship of the personae of new gods, mainly the Sun God Tezcatlipoca, the Smoking Mirror, seems to imply a change in the ideological fabric. It suggests that from that moment they were able to accept ideas not linked directly with agriculture. Most likely the new gods were tribal totemic divinities, probably the deifications of former leaders from whom the Toltecs claimed descent.

In the legends of the fall of Tula, the ancient religions and the new ones come into conflict in several ways. In one, the local ruler, Topiltzin, Our Lord, is led by Tezcatlipocas's wiles to violate saintly conduct and, in shame, goes away. In another the two gods, personified by dual rulers that bear their names, fight each other, and Tezcatlipoca emerges the winner. Quetzalcoatl, with his host, retires to Tlillan Tlapallan, the Place of the Black and the Red, toward the East, warning that he will come back, a prophecy that became very relevant when the

Spanish arrived some five hundred years later.

But the clearest example of this dialectic is in another tradition—the Ball Game. The Mesoamerican game is one of many sports that were played with rubber balls in the New World and that are still played, in different ways, in several places in Mexico and the southwestern United States. The Toltec version was played in a long H-shaped court with the middle line serving as the pitch. It seems to have been played without hands, using mainly the shoulders and hips to propel a solid rubber ball through a hoop in the middle of the court. It was popular throughout Mesoamerica beginning in late Formative times, or about 500 B.C. Strangely, though, Teotihuacán does not have a formalized ball game building for there the game was played with wooden posts for goals, as shown in a mural painting.

The Ball Game also seems to have been an occasion for betting, for spectators and players alike, and was sometimes very important as a religious ceremony, with sides

Figure 34. A hard rubber ball had to be hit by the elbow, wrist, or hip through one of the two stone rings.

Figure 35. The Great Ball Court at Chitzén Itzá was 480 feet long and 120 feet wide. (William M. Ferguson and John Q. Royce, *Maya Ruins of Mexico in Color*)

representing day and night, light and darkness, or life and death. Some modern writers, with more drama than truth, have claimed that the losing team—or sometimes the winning team—were ceremonially sacrificed after a match.

According to legend, the Toltec ruler was so powerful that he boastfully challenged the water gods to a match. He won and, as a prize, claimed their treasures of greenstone, turquoise, and gold. In revenge they withdrew their rain, and the city had to succumb.

How Tula really came to fall as a great city is not known. It did not disappear as a settlement, and certainly was a town important enough later so that an Aztec king's daughter married its ruler. The site has important buildings from periods that date after its mythical ending. Nevertheless, it seems eventually to have ceased to be a powerful force, and its fall may have been connected with the wanderings of Nahuatl-speaking tribes, one of which may have been the later powerful Aztec.

All the World Is Aztec Land

When the Aztec became strong enough, one of their rulers ordered that every book that dealt with their history be burned and new ones be written so as to show the glory of his people since all the world belonged to them. Thus the people that met the European conquerors were able to invent their own past. This is not a unique feat in history, but our own inquisitive need for knowing the real story has not been helped by it.

They claimed to have come from Aztlán, the Place of Cranes, somewhere in the north, led by four God-Bearers, together with six other

9

Figure 36. This famous sculpture, found accidentally during the laying of cable for the Mexico City telephone system, is one of the masterworks of Aztec art. It represents Coyolxauhqui, the sister of the Aztec tribal god Huitzilopochtli. According to legend, she harassed their mother and was killed and dismembered by Huitzilopochtli. (Photo by C. Alcazar, *Historia del arte mexicano* SALVAT 2:55)

Nahuatl-speaking groups. They told of their deeds in their long pilgrimage, when their tribal god, Huitzilopochtli, the Left-Handed Hummingbird, told them not to settle permanently until they reached a place in the middle of a lake where, on a stone, an eagle, Huitzilopochtli's totemic sign, would be seen devouring a serpent, the old god Quetzalcoatl's emblem.

Their trek had many stops and many battles. After overcoming the temptation to stay put in several places, they finally reached the foretold spot and there they founded, under their chieftain Tenoch, Cactus on a Stone, the city of Tenochtitlán, in his name. This was Mexico City, later the center of Anahuac, the known world, the land around water. There they grew powerful until they could conquer the Valley of Mexico, and from that base they became the overlords, the feeders of the gods.

That is the Aztec tradition and, like many official traditions, it contains more than slight exaggeration. The city could hardly have been founded by the Aztec. Proof is abundant of its having been inhabited prior to their founding date of A.D. 1325. Formative Period figurines from about 1000 B.C. were found during excavations for the building of the Latin American Tower, one of downtown Mexico City's tallest edifices; these figurines can still be seen in the tower's observation room on the fiftieth floor. Teotihuacán remains have been found, though without good controls, within city limits. While the cathedral was being repaired, in the 1970s, archaeological excavations were carried out and pottery from about A.D. 1000 to 1100 was found.

More important, in Tlatelolco, about a mile north of the center of the city, while a subway station was under construction, evidence was unearthed for a settlement from about A.D. 1100. Tlatelolco and Tenochtitlán were small, neighboring islands in one of the lakes

Figure 37. This large stone conch was dug at the site of the Aztec Templo Mayor (main temple) at Tenochtitlán, the Aztec capital, where economic and military power met religious and administrative centralization. This great, teeming metropolis awed the Spanish conquerors. (*Historia del arte mexicano* SALVAT 2:32)

that covered the central part of the Valley of Mexico until the final part of the nineteenth century, when it was finally drained. Tlatelolco, the Place of the Earth Mound, seems to have been an important market center for the Valley long before the date the Aztec claim they got there.

The Aztec themselves could well have come, as they said, from the north, and some authors place their origin in the south of the state of Guanajuato in northcentral Mexico, or from the west, from the state of Nayarit. (There is no evidence for their having come from California.) They could just as well have been another of the many farmer groups that settled in the Valley for thousands of years, acquired their ethnic characteristics after the fall of Teotihuacán, and were able to survive the chaos after Tula's demise. Their culture shows a typical Mesoamerican life with one difference: in their central compound they kept a patch of ground arranged with cacti and stones to remind them of the northern desert.

Otherwise, though, their cultural traits were those of their neighbors:

their pottery, Tenochtitlán Black-on-Orange, is a variant of an earlier ware, Tenayuca Black-on-Orange, which was widely distributed in the Valley until fashion changed and the new design was introduced. Cholula Polychrome, also associated with them, was an imported ceramic ware that had a wide distribution for some two hundred years before the Aztec came forth. It is also associated with other types, from the south and west, like Tlahuica Polychrome and Tenango Brown-on-Tan.

Their double temples on top of pyramids, dedicated, respectively, to the Rain God and to their tribal hero, although not found in Toltec construction, were common in the Valley of Mexico long before the Aztecs arrived. They were erected in other places as well, like Tenayuca and Santa Cecilia, north of Mexico City, where well-preserved and restored buildings still can be seen. Human sacrifices, of course, had been common earlier, although the Aztecs performed this ritual on a much larger scale. Their god, Huitzilopochtli, was their own version of Tezcatlipoca, whom they also worshiped, but other groups had equivalent tribal ancestors as deities.

The story about their conquests, on the other hand, is mostly true. After taking over the Valley by forming an alliance with two other towns, Tlacopan and Texcoco, they extended their domain to most of Central Mexico and south to the confines of the Maya area. Their city grew to a size and magnificence that astounded the Europeans who saw it, and they established an empire that was sustained by tribute paid in large quantities and by trade channeled through the Tlatelolco market.

Aztec conquest and its consequent tribute brought to their city many riches, which made it a highly cosmopolitan settlement very much like Teotihuacán. Goods from many provinces were brought in for payment of taxes, and these were exchanged in the market for other merchandise and re-exported to far places. The distribution of Tenochtitlán Black-on-Orange and Cholula Polychrome throughout Mesoamerica is witness to their activity.

Figure 38. Mitla, a Late Postclassic site in Oaxaca, was inhabited at the time of the conquest. Its walls are famous for their decoration. In local lore Mitla was associated with the underworld and the souls of the dead. (Photo by William M. Ferguson and John Q. Royce)

Their splendor was not limited to goods but included the use of human beings on a gigantic scale. The tribute they received in labor enabled them to build huge public works and private palaces. Caravans of hundreds of human carriers moved through the city. Prisoners from many wars were brought for sacrifice; with their blood and hearts the gods, especially the sun, could be fed and thus the universe kept from collapsing again, as the Aztecs believed it had already done four times before present mankind was placed on earth. Ambassadors from many towns came to be awed by the spectacle; they returned to their lands with the message that it made sense to acknowledge Aztec might.

Aztec strength had its limits, though, and the Spanish conquerors seized on these weaknesses. Distance, as with Teotihuacán's domain, was one. The empire stretched so far that it was hard to control it. Some part or another was constantly in rebellion and the central government had to intervene in innumerable local wars if it was to remain dominant. An efficient messenger service had to be established to carry news to the central government by relays of runners. These served to advise Moctezuma of the arrival of the Europeans but were not enough to raise the countryside to the defense of the capital.

Military organization was another shortcoming. The Aztec empire was based on military rule and paid for it by having to garrison provinces and borders. Roads had to be patrolled and caravans protected. The army was not enough for the task, and more and more of the work had to be carried out by Otomi mercenaries who, when the time came, did not defend Mexico City from the Europeans. Unconquered groups, like the Tarascan in the West, the Mixtec in the South, or the Tlaxcaltec, uncomfortably near their heartland, had to be continually fought and contained. With the coming of the Spanish, some groups saw their opportunity to defeat the Aztecs. The Tlaxcaltec became their allies; others did not resist them.

Social imbalance was one more weakness. With the growth of the

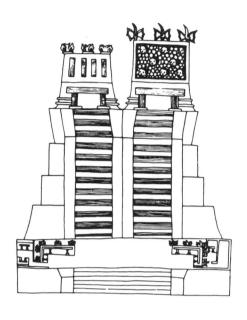

empire, the original nobility was unable to cope with the job of administration, yet they continued to do so until the end of the fifteenth century. By that time the work of running the world was so big that the Aztec ruler Ahuizotl started appointing commoners to high posts. An enormous bureaucracy resulted. At his death his successor, Moctezuma, after putting down many local revolts, tried to reverse this policy. When the Spanish arrived, though, the reorganization had not been completed. This transitional situation greatly helped them.

Political entanglements were probably decisive, too. The original alliance of the Aztec with Texcoco and

Figure 39. The Great Temple of the Aztecs towered 135 feet high and dominated the ancient ceremonial center of Tenochtitlán. The Spaniards built over the sacred site in creating today's Mexico City, but between 1978 and 1982 the area was excavated.

Tlacopán developed into a fine game of intervention politics. Zones of influence were always contested, and finally the Aztec were able to determine their allied rulers' succession by forcing the election of their preferred candidates. At the arrival of the Spanish, opposition had developed and, in Texcoco it was decisive in allowing the Europeans time and resources for the siege of Mexico City.

The Aztec had really fallen into a trap of their own making. In achieving their greatness, they became too large and prepared their own downfall. Their conquests, which they themselves believed were holy quests, were only futile movements in an unending and hopeless cycle for survival. Their first conquest, the Valley of Mexico, had subjected a number of towns that produced the same goods as the Aztecs themselves. When the produce came to market as tribute, it competed ruinously against the Aztec farmer. All movements after that were ill-fated.

Their next conquest was the Valley of Morelos and the Balsas River region to the south, which brought them cotton, cacao, copper, and gold, goods that were used as coinage in pre-Hispanic Mexico, which unbalanced the market further. The solution might have been, perhaps, a period of peace, to enable them to digest and adapt to the new scale of their economy, but instead they embarked on successive enterprises, each of which progressively weakened their real power. At the arrival of the Europeans, regardless of the Aztecs' apparent grandeur, they were in disarray.

The End and
a New Beginning

When the Spanish came, the power
of the Aztec empire was breaking. The
Tarascans had stopped their advance
and counterattacked successfully,
which forced the Aztecs to hold a line
of forts in order to resist their
offensive. It did not work. Oztuma, in
the state of Guerrero, their main base,
was overrun, and the foe would have
become a real menace if he pressed
that advantage. In the South, Oaxaca,
a garrison town meant to protect that
part of the empire, was being looked
upon more and more as a possible
capital for the southern half of a split
empire. Distance would have made

10

thio move necessary. The arrival of the Europeans barred this from happening.

For the Mesoamerican archaeological sequence, the Aztec represent another phase in the integration and disintegration of a territorial unit. Because of the size of their empire, it became too large for their culture or technology to rule successfully. In a way, their history and the magnificence of their empire are only anecdotes in this process. For us, however, they are more than that. The Aztec are the first of the high-culture groups that met European expansion; therefore, what happened to them and to their conquerors is also a part of our history in the Western world.

The Spanish conquest, then, besides being the product of the unquestioned military and political genius of Hernán Cortés, was also a product of internal conditions in the Aztec domain. Its development is interesting. After being well received by Moctezuma, who thought they might have been Quetzalcoatl's host returning to fulfill his prophecy, the Spanish were attacked and forced to retreat from the

Figure 40. Detail from a post-Conquest drawing showing Hernán Cortés and Malinche, his Indian concubine, meeting Moctezuma (seated). Malinche served as translator, advisor, and mistress, and today in Mexico her name has passed into infamy with the meaning "turncoat."

Figure 41. The Spaniards with their Indian allies are shown here attacking The Great Temple of the Aztecs at Tenochtitlán. It took Cortés just over two years from his arrival in Mexico to complete his conquest in August 1521. (Eric Wolf, *Sons of the Shaking Earth*)

city. What followed was a masterpiece of reorganization and training of native allied forces and a siege.

This final episode, launched with only flat-bottomed sailing brigantines built out of the remains of the Spanish fleet (which had been scuttled to prevent retreat) is one of the most interesting naval operations in history. It required the blockading of the city, the interception of forces trying to assist in its defense from outside, and frequent landings to harass its defenders, who finally, after some seventy-five days, had to surrender. It ranks with the two other great naval battles of the sixteenth century, Lepanto, where the Spanish and the Venetians defeated the Turks, and the sinking of the Spanish Armada by the English. Both sides have told their versions of the saga.

But even the Spanish conquest itself is only heroic adventure. The important part is the contact of the two cultures—Mesoamerican and European—and eventually their mutual enrichment, albeit with sad and bloody consequences initially.

One tends to think of Spain, even at

that time, as a modern country. It is not that good an image. The Iberian Peninsula had been a field of battle for eight centuries in a war that resulted in the expansion of one of its component kingdoms, Castile, until it became paramount in the West in alliance with Aragon, to the East, after the marriage of their rulers, Isabella and Ferdinand. This alliance respected each kingdom's independence and spheres of influence. As a consequence, Spain developed two policies: Aragon remained a Mediterranean power while Castile saw itself primarily as a force in the Atlantic.

Its own ethnic integration was by no means complete when it took on the conquest of the Indies. Divided, from the northern Basques to the southern Andalusians, it had recently expelled, in 1492, two of its most important groups—Moors and Jews. Spanish society had not fully absorbed the consequences. Since Spain's experience with foreign peoples had been almost exclusively with the conquest of these two peoples, its first reaction to dealing with the strange, unclad Indians of America had been to reproduce the institutions and laws that were thought to have been successful with the Moors and the Jews. These policies were to be revised later when the New World proved to be quite different from the Old World.

The Spanish monarchy was engaged, as were many others in its time, in a campaign to enhance its own power against that of feudal barons. The end of the Middle Ages was not just a matter of painters and sculptors but, ofttimes, a bloody fight for the acceptance of royal authority. King Ferdinand had fought the final battles, but the war was not over. The newly conquered continent offered many opportunities for the rebirth of feudalism, and Spanish royal policy had to be designed to prevent this from happening.

So was born the encomienda, the system that bonded the Indians to a Spaniard, who undertook in return to Christianize them and teach them the Spanish language. In payment he was granted the product of their labor. The system, of course, lent itself to abuse. Interminable law suits were fought to curb the power of its beneficiaries until it finally disappeared after more than a century.

Furthermore, with a Spanish family, the Borgias, controlling the papacy, the country was drawn into church politics. The history of the conquest of America was, in many ways, the story of quarrels between monastic orders to acquire territory and prerogatives and to exclude their competitors in salvation. The crown's decision to allow, at the beginning, only Franciscans and Dominicans in its new lands was very important in the way the cultures met. The church's position was determined through even the choosing of many of the first missionaries from among the Belgian, Portuguese, and others, rather than from just Spanish subjects of the imperial government.

Figure 42. The fortress-like convent at Acolmán, in the Valley of Mexico, is a good example of early colonial construction for the use of Indian populations recently converted to Christianity. It was built for the Augustine Order. (Photo by William M. Ferguson and John Q. Royce)

Figure 43. A sixteenth-century *atrio* cross at the Augustinian church of San Agustín. The style has great similarities with pre-Columbian relief carving and represents a merging of the Indian with the Spanish style. The relief carving represented the Passion of Christ, using symbols such as the palm branch, ladder, and crown of thorns, so that the Indians would not identify it with human sacrifice. (Photo by Mary Grizzard)

The introduction, later, of other orders and nonmonastic clergy was a major shift in policy necessitated by the European political situation and the rise of Protestantism. These developments affected important changes in the process of Christianization and settlement of America. Expansion toward the North, the Mexican Northwest and the United States, required different strategies, and these were entrusted to other missionaries, like the Jesuits, who looked very differently at the problem of pagans and heretics.

So the two cultures met. The contact was made at all levels and meant many things. Though we can be quite confused by looking at specific events and even take sides with the Indians or the Spanish, the processes of contact and conquest certainly were neither easy nor quick. They involved battles and massacres as well as episodes of profound charity and goodness. They also meant deep change for everyone involved— Europeans as well as natives. Both spheres became inextricably entangled

with each other and have remained so
to the present.

What did European conquest mean
to Mesoamerica? We would tend to
look mostly at biological mixing, the
Christian religion, Spanish suzerainty,
the Castilian language—all of them
acquired by the Indians. A deeper
analysis would probably point toward
the wheel, animals such as the bull
and the horse to carry and pull, pigs,
goats, and chickens, iron tools, the
plow, wheat, and other plants as the
main contributions that changed the
Mesoamerican way of life. They were
not only the consequences of conquest
but also its agents, and they have
become permanent elements—
structurally important parts—in the
way the American continent has
evolved since the sixteenth century.

What about the other side? What
did Mesoamerica have to give to the
European world as a reward for
conquest? Untold riches in silver and
other metals, labor, and a field for
opportunity come immediately to
mind. But look at the catsup in your
hamburger or the chili in your chili
con carne; see your children chewing

Figure 44. Indian tributaries of Mexico are shown working in the garden of a Spaniard in the vicinity of the city about 1565. Various of the plants being tended were introduced from the Old World. The wooden spade (upper right) is of prehispanic origin, while the hoe (lower right) is Spanish. (H. R. Harvey and Hanns J. Prem, *Explorations in Ethnohistory*)

gum or eating chocolate or peanut butter; smoke a cigarette; eat a nice Christmas dinner with turkey; munch on popcorn; or dine on steak from cornfed cattle—do any of these and you will start to grasp the contributions of Mesoamerica to the rest of the world.

In the world of ideas, Mesoamerica made its mark, but its impact was limited because of European ethnocentrism. It served as the launching pad to yet another part of the world—East Asia, Japan, China, and the Philippines were discovered on voyages from Mexican ports. Their culture was sifted through Mesoamerica on its way to Europe. But many of Mesoamerica's ideas went unused because Europe was not prepared for them; however, it would have been even more enriched by the contact had it done so.

Some Suggested Reading

You may want to read more on this subject. The list that follows presents some of the most interesting books that try to sum up and systematize the story of Mesoamerica. They do not duplicate one another, nor do they even make good substitutes for each other. Each one tells a different story, since they concentrate on different aspects, depending on what their authors consider most important or see as the basic problem.

Their authors represent the best of research into the Mesoamerican past available in English. There are many other scholars writing on specific subjects in field reports or dissertations whose works are not included in this short list for obvious reasons. They are well worth reading, however, since our syntheses are based on their work.

Some of the authors on this list will surely disagree with some of my points of view. It will be an honor for me to discuss these disagreements with my former teachers and present friends.

Bernal, Ignacio. *Mexico Before Cortez.* New York, 1975.

Coe, Michael D. *Mexico.* New York, 1977.

———. *The Maya.* New York, 1980.

Horcasitas, Fernando. *The Aztecs, Then and Now.* Mexico City, 1979.

Sanders, William, and Price, Barbara J. *Mesoamerica: The Evolution of a Civilization.* New York, 1968.

Willey, Gordon R. *An Introduction to American Archaeology.* 2 vols. Englewood Cliffs, N.J., 1966, 1971.

Weaver, Muriel Porter. *The Aztecs, the Maya, and Their Predecessors.* New York, 1972.

Wolf, Eric R. *Sons of the Shaking Earth.* Chicago, 1959.

Index

People from the Land of
  Rubber, 23
Peten sites, 51
physical traits, 7, 25
pigment, 66
Place of the Black and the
  Red, 93
Place of Cranes, 97
Place of the Earth Mounds,
  102
Place Where Gods Were
  Made, The, 43
plants, used by man, 12, 13
Plumbate ware, 70, 81
pochteca, 31
politics, 109, 120
populations, 36, 76
potato, 12
pottery, 13, 25, 39, 47, 66,
  69, 70, 71, 74, 87, 88, 89,
  100, 103, 104
power, 46, 47, 50
Puebla-Tlaxcala valley, 63
Putuns, the, 77
Puuc phase, 79
pyramids, 26, 37, 43, 57, 63,
  90, 103

Queretaro, the state of, 87
Quetzalcoatl, 46, 93, 99, 114
Quintana Roo, the state of,
  66

Rain God, 43, 63, 103
religion, 26, 36, 43, 76, 93,
94; ceremonial centers, 29,
  36; the church, 120–23;
  spiritual life, 18

San Lorenzo site, 29
Santa Cecilia site, 103
Santa Isabel Ixtapán site, 9
Sayil site, 66
sculpture, 57, 90; stone
  heads, 25
Seibal site, 77
Serpent of Smoke, 84
settlement, 36
Smoking Mirror, 93
social organization, 46, 107,
  118; civilization, 31, 37;
  distances, 47, 50–51, 106;
  encomienda, 119; farmers,
  12, 16, 102, 110;
  feudalism, 119; hunters,
  5, 9, 12, 66, 71, 77, 84, 90;
  idle time, 13; metropolis,
  37, 47; power, 46, 47, 50;
  settlement, 36; symbols of
  rank, 31; unification, 70
South America, 12
southwest, the American, 9,
  39, 71, 84, 94
Spain, 117–19
Spanish, the, 94, 106, 107,
  109, 110, 113, 114–23
specialization, 16–18
spiritual life, 18. *See also*
  religion
squash, 13